THE STATE VISIT
DRAMA

Kraftgriots

Also in the series (DRAMA)

Rasheed Gbadamosi: *Trees Grow in the Desert*
Rasheed Gbadamosi: *3 Plays*
Akomaye Oko: *The Cynic*
Chris Nwamuo: *The Squeeze & Other Plays*
Olu Obafemi: *Naira Has No Gender*
Chinyere Okafor: *Campus Palavar & Other Plays*
Chinyere Okafor: *The Lion and the Iroko*
Ahmed Yerima: *The Silent Gods*
Ebereonwu: *Cobweb Seduction*
Ahmed Yerima: *Kaffir's Last Game*
Ahmed Yerima: *The Bishop & the Soul* with *Thank You Lord*
Ahmed Yerima: *The Trials of Oba Ovoramwen*
Ahmed Yerima: *Attahiru*
Ahmed Yerima: *The Sick People* (2000)
Omome Anao: *Lions at War & Other Plays* (2000)
Ahmed Yerima: *Dry Leaves on Ukan Trees* (2001)
Ahmed Yerima: *The Sisters* (2001)

THE STATE VISIT
DRAMA

Niyi Osundare

kraftgriots

Published by

Kraft Books Limited
6A Polytechnic Road, Sango, Ibadan
Box 22084, University of Ibadan Post Office,
Ibadan, Oyo State, Nigeria
℡ 234 (02) 8106655
E-mail: krabooks@onebox.com

© Niyi Osundare 2002

First published 2002

ISBN 978–039–058–8

= KRAFTGRIOTS =
(A literary imprint of Kraft Books Limited)

All Rights Reserved

First printing, February 2002

Computer typeset on 10 point charter typeface by
MOWA COMPUTERS, Ibadan

Characters

Narrator
Head
Minister of Finance
Minister of External Affairs
Minister of Public Morality
Minister of Agriculture

Sule
Etim } Beggars
Obi
Abeke

Alms-giver
Journalist
Professor
Medalsmith
Colonel Anapa
Painter
Policeman
Old man
Student
Worker
Soldiers, Guards, Whip-carriers, Street Decorators, Crowd

This play was first produced by THE CREATIVITY WORKSHOP, at the Arts Theatre, University of Ibadan, Nigeria, January 10 through 12, 1997. It was directed by Wale Oyinlola, with the following cast:

Narrator	Charles Ihimodu
Head	Adebisi Ademakinwa
Finance I	Ben Iwuala
Finance II	Emmanuel Ekong
Ext. Affairs	Ifeanyi Ogu
Public Morality	Bisola Oke-Davies
Agriculture	Ademola Ogundele
Sule	Ignatius Oginni
Etim	Jide Fadiya
Obi	Lawson Ochonogor
Abeke	Iyabo Ajibola & Ekaite Bassey
Alms-giver	Rosemary Itam
Journalist	Lekan Fagbade
Professor	Adikiba Boyle
Medalsmith	Abiodun Akharume
Colonel Anapa	Rowland Ogidan
Painter	Abiodun Akharume
Policeman	Abiodun Akharume
Old man	Ademola Ogundele
Student	Jide Fadiya
Workers	Gafar Ajao, Ignatius Oginni, Ekaite Bassey
Soldiers	Matthew Obot & Others
Sergeant	Kola Apantaku
Guard	Gafar Ajao
Inspector	Ben Iwuala
Masses	Cast

Production Crew

Props	Jide Fadiya
Costumes & Make-up	Rosemary Itam
Set & Lights	Ademola Adetunji
Stage Manager	Emeka Aboh
Director	Wale Oyinloia

I gratefully acknowledge the contributions of these young women and men to the final outcome of this play, and commend the vision and courage of the Director, Wale Oyinlola, who flew the production in the face of one of the most repressive military dictatorships in Nigeria's history.

Act I

The stage is set for a State Cabinet meeting. Downstage centre, the Head of State is seated on a throne-like chair with a prominent backrest and gold-plated arm rests. The Head (as he enjoys being called) is chronically obese, and slumps in his monumental chair breathing hard. He is in army uniform, preferably fatigue but his hat is placed on the table before him, while the belt disappears in the generous folds of flesh making up his abdomen.

Directly before the Head, the Ministers sit face-to-face behind a table or tables littered with dog-eared files, red tapes sticking conspicuously out of them. The entire chamber reeks of decadent affluence.

The national armorial bearing, placed on the back wall behind and above the Head, depicts a running lion with a prey in its mouth.

The two side doors to the chamber are guarded by two hefty soldiers in full combat fatigue, guns at the ready.

The Narrator, who all the while has been sitting among the audience, springs to his feet, proclaims his lines as he picks his way dignifiedly between the rows of seats, and heads for the stage. The house lights fade to black. Spotlight falls on Narrator as he becomes more deliberate, more expansive in his rendering, talking directly with the audience. The Cabinet is frozen in semi-darkness.

NARRATOR: There is a Land of Two Rivers, a land blessed with milk and honey, the softest and the healthiest of sunshine. But a few men fouled up the milk, and mixed the honey with cow-dung. Men who have power to act and not be questioned: men who measure their own height by the genuflection of others.

How many, oh how many shall we count
Of the teeth of Adepele:
There are twenty incisors, fifty canines,

While uncountable molars lie buried
In the caves of the jaw

(*Pause*) As I was saying, this land is rich in everything. But the wealth is in the hands of a few kings and queens. The only possession the people have in abundance is poverty. When asked to abolish it, the kings say that p-o-v-e-r-t-y is a seven-letter word, a sacred number that no God-fearing nation can ever afford to miss. So the wealthy fester in opulence, the poor squirm in their poverty.

The flashiest of foreign cars find their destination in the Land of Two Rivers: the Cadillac hurries through the assembly line abroad to join the queue in its cities, the Jaguar finds a resting place in its private garages; the Mercedes glides in, a glossy wonder. The last brand has been so long with us that it even has a stanza in the poetry of opulence (*sings and dances*):

Mèsí Olóyè, oba okò
Ayókélé wolé olówó òtá òtòsì
Mèsí Olóyè, sunbèbè sókè wóóóróóó
Ó sèdí ràbàtà bí àlè ogun odun
Mèsí niran, ta ló ní kò niran,
N bó rodo tálákà nílè
Ngbà tó ya òdò olówó
Òtòsì tó rí Mèsí ti ò sá
Ara ikú ló nya
Tani ò mò pé táyà Mèsí wooo lórí tálákà
Kí nsegbé eni alábaun tè látèpa
Ijó nbá kú, kàkà kí nkú jífà
Edùmàrè bá nwá bee Mèsí sun dandan*

(*Wipes his face: smiles a wry, knowing smile*). Yes, everybody plucks a feather off the eagle, then wonders why the national bird has failed to fly. Governments award emergency contracts for bridges which collapse under the first bicycle. You and I may complain about a broken bridge: as for the kings — and queens — no problem: no broken bridge hinders their helicopter in the sky ... well, unless it is the one between here and Switzerland. The doctor takes egg bribes from kwashiorkor patients, his stethoscope placed on the pulse of his bank account: the magistrate counts justice in notes and coins; the guilty buy innocence from the courts as tender for public office.

How many, oh how many can we count ...?

The journalist turns a mere minion for looting — oh did I say "loot"? — I mean ruling powers. He dips his pen in the slime of falsehood and his vision trips on the plane of History. His throat cleared by constant inducement, he bombards the public's ear with official lies.

And the middlemen of business who stand between us and progress: buying cheap, selling dear, smuggling, hoarding, extorting, crushing under the weight of profit: forwarders and backwarders, manufacturers' representatives, habitual slavers who haggle away our freedom just like their fathers, their fathers' fathers, their fathers' fathers' fathers

How many, oh how many ...?

The policeman who flogs bribes out of mere suspects; the port worker who makes cargo disappear through the talisman of tricks: the clergy who breaks into holy sweat after swallowing all the widow's mite; the university don who pawns his wife for a chair

How many, oh how many ...?

Some know these problems exist but are too comfortable to stir: some hastily conclude that it is all God's design. Of those who care, many do not know what to do. They wring their fingers, shake their heads, explode loud hisses, and grumble. But there is a few who know that silence and acquiescence are the tonic of oppression; that they are the nurturers of tyranny, who flatter when they should kick; they bequeath a dumb future who take asking questions as an act of treason. *(Takes a pensive pause; shakes head in sagely manner.)* But o too! Loquacity, they say, is the father of lies. I have said enough; now let us act the rest. Let us see how our looters — oh that word again! — prepare for the visit of one of their friends across the border.

Lights slowly reveal the cabinet which goes into action immediately. First, they sing the National Anthem a copy of which is boldly displayed on a board stage-front where it can be clearly read by the audience. It can also be beamed through the use of an overhead projector.

    Land of the Lion, Land of the Strong
    Land of the Righteous, we sing your song
    Striving every moment, day and night
    The world must bow beneath your might

    Land of Plenty, Land of Wealth
    Showered with blessing, the best of health
    We carry our fate in our very hand
    Backward never on Yankeland

    Equal Justice, equal Peace
    On our stainless banner the centre piece
    A Land awash with honey and milk
    Where every robe is sumptuous silk

    Land of the Lion with Powerful claws
    Known everywhere for its gentle laws
    Yankeans arise to the noble call
    Build a nation that is free for all

HEAD: Ladies and gentlemen — oh *(laughs raucously)* there is only one lady here ... *(others join in the laughter)*, well, you know why we are here today. As our people say, unless there is a solid reason, a woman does not bear the name

"Kumolu". A brother head of state from the Republic of Wilama is paying us a state visit next month. He is a man who needs no introduction: Son of the Leopard, Descendant of the Towering Giraffe. Offshoot of a warrior family, his father fought the Arobela, killing thousands and enslaving twice as many. These slaves he sold to white men from across the seas, who gave him beads for his crown, bottles of gin, little mirrors, and the money upon which his royal wealth is based. *(The Ministers explode into shouts of approbation: "Dansaki! Ranka dede! Omenuko! Ogbeni Ogun!)*

And as a true son of his father, the President of Wilama has steered the ship of state along the turbulent seas of our time. As a benevolent leader of his people, he banned parliament, preferring the direct rule of his family to the endless bickerings of that house of words where the only thing that gets done is nothing. Believing as we here do that opposition is injurious to good governance, he burnt down unfriendly media houses and dumped vocal critics in some safe prison behind the hills where they receive a real royal treatment! *(Again, wild laughter amid roars of approbation from the Cabinet)*

Realising the importance of marriage in uniting the country, he commanded each tribal chief to donate a virgin to his royal harem.

PUBLIC MORALITY: *(Interjecting)* Ah! Ṣọ̀pọ̀hnọ́ o! that is an impossible task these days: virgins are more rare than gold!

(General laughter)

HEAD: *(Continuing)* To stop tribal rivalries, he brought in expatriates to head all the corporations in Wilama. He imported a teacher from a Manchester High School in England to head the only university in the country. No nation except ours has been more stable, more prosperous, more peaceful, more progressive. This is why we must do everything to give this august visitor the fitting welcome he deserves. Our reputation as hospitable people is at stake. Our nation is at stake. We ourselves are at stake.

(Another roar of approbation, then the Cabinet "debate".)

PUB. MORALITY: Our Head, Father of the Nation, our most beloved leader, God-fearing, God-chosen to rule ... you have spoken well. But money says: "let nobody make any plans without me". How much are we budgeting for this great visit?

HEAD: Good question. Minister of Finance, how much can you spare for this visit?

FINANCE: You should be asking how much altogether we have in the treasury. The decline in the production of cocoa, coffee, and tea has depleted our national earnings. Add to these the drought and famine of recent months ... We are barely managing ...

AGRIC: Yes, you know I complain every time. These farmers are growing lazy when they should be growing crops.

FINANCE: But don't you think they are old too? Many of these farmers are so old their backs are bent like ancient bows. And farming is so tedious, so unprofitable, that the young ones are running away from it.

AGRIC: That is not the reason. They are just lazy *(pronounced 'lasy')*. They are against the progressive programmes of this government.

FINANCE: That's not true. They ...

AGRIC: I have never lied in my life *(pause)* unless it is absolutely necessary. See, many of these farmers are subfer *(has problems pronouncing the word correctly)* ... subfasif. They are being used by agents from Russia, China and, and, and *(pause)* Switzerland.

FINANCE: Ooooooh! So five years ago when locusts devastated the land, the farmers caused it? And last year's prolonged drought, did not farmers cause it too? When things were so bad that not a single speck of green was left on the field, and even the farmers and their families starved for months. And, of course, the relief materials, the fertilisers earmarked for the farmers, where did they go?

AGRIC: Un hun, don't point an accusing finger at me o. *Àbí*, each of us knows how we run our ministries. *Àbí?*

EXT. AFFAIRS: As a matter of fact and protocol, this is really not my field. I'm used to settling quarrels among nations ... but our Head, our gracious leader, we must put an end to this squabble before it develops into something else.

HEAD: Yes, yes. Let us not dig up useless old quarrels when we have a pressing job in hand. Or we may be like that man who leaves his leprosy to spread while busy chasing a cure for his craw-craw.

PUB. MORALITY: Aaaaha! You have said everything!

HEAD: Finance, how much do we have for this visit?

FINANCE: I don't know ... but I know we have two hundred million arina altogether in the treasury.

AGRIC: *(On warpath again)* Aaaah ha! How do you count your own money — forward or backward? I thought it was five hundred million arina last week.

FINANCE: Ask the Head. He drew three hundred million three days ago without my knowledge.

(All eyes turn to Head)

HEAD: Yes, yes, yes ... it is true. We used it to buy a jet fighter from a friendly country.

EXT. AFFAIRS: But we are not at war. Indeed, we have the reputation of being the most peaceful country in the world...

HEAD: *(Cutting in)* Yes, but we need weapons of war to maintain our peace. You see, peace is like a machine: if you don't service it with jets and tanks and armoured cars, it breaks down irreparably. Aaah! *Agbagaaa!* *(shakes his head in a mock-sagacious manner).* As our people say, *kó'jú maa rí 'bi, ęsę lòògun rę.*

AGRIC: *(Cutting in)* My Head, *gbogbo ara loògun rę.*

ALL THE MINISTERS EXCEPT FINANCE: Good word, Lion of Yanke! Absolute truth!

HEAD: So, Finance, what is the true amount in your account?

FINANCE: I have said it: two hundred million

HEAD: We shall need two hundred million more.

FINANCE: Aaah! ... but ...

HEAD: But but, but is the beat of the butt *(laughs self-indulgently).* Yes, you see, people accuse us these days of talking in terms of millions and billions. They don't know that everything has gone up. And as those troublemakers in our university like saying, the only thing that goes up in Yanke without ever coming down is prices. Eeeeh? Even our prostitutes now charge higher. I heard one of them singing the other day *(walks right to the centre of the stage, laughing and gesticulating wildly as he sings):*

Isú gbówó nèrí	(The price of yam has gone up)
Ògèdè gbówó nèrí	(The price of plantain has gone up)
Abęrę dókítà gbówó nèrí	(The doctor's needle is now expensive)
Pankéèkì gbówó nèrí	(Even pancake has gone up in price)

(Now pointing lasciviously to the region between his thighs)

Ó yę kí tibi náà gbówó nèrí	(This one too should raise its price)

(The Cabinet laughs wildly as if their job depends on it)
You see, there are places in this country today where they now take television, refrigerator, and motor cycles as bride price. Our people are moving fast; we the government must learn to keep pace.

FINANCE: How do we come about the extra amount?

HEAD: Borrow it from a friendly nation. Take it from America *(pronounced "Amorika")*. America will give you anything as long as you promise to have nothing to do with the Russians.

AGRIC: They are also very generous with their wheat. And their powdered milk, the one our people call America-do-me-good.

PUB. MORALITY: *(Covering her mouth with her handkerchief)* Un un un! The one that makes you fart like a hippopotamus! I understand that is what they give to dogs in their own country.(General laughter. Agric, completely carried away falls over Public Morality, narrowly missing her breasts. She seizes Agric's fingers and twists them, while the erring Minister howls like a wounded lion. The other Ministers rock with more laughter. Only the Minister of Finance keeps a straight face, his hands folded across his chest.)*

FINANCE: *(When the uproar has finally died down)* I'm not saying we shouldn't go begging again, but this time what shall we say we need the money for?

AGRIC: An urgent state business.

FINANCE: Remember just last year we borrowed two hundred million dollars from ...

HEAD: We did not borrow it. America gave it to us as "thank you" money for allowing them to use Biirona as military base. We can always ask them for more. They are our friends.

FINANCE: Our masters! Debtors and creditors are never equals. Debts, debts. Debts eat away our freedom. Debts enslave our future.

AGRIC: You can pour as much *ewi* as your throat will allow. What future are you talking about? The future is not the problem now. When it comes it will take care of itself. Let us eat and be merry today. Why should we bother about tomorrow? You can only grab what you see.

PUB. MORALITY: *(With the enthusiasm of someone who has just made a monumental discovery)* I have an idea. *(Pause)* Let us print more money!

(A general roar of approval)

AGRIC: Oh Morality! Trust you to come out always with new ideas! *Agbagaa!* I am sure all your children are male! Yes, that is wonderful. How can we say there is no money when we can produce millions and millions by decree? Afterall, we control the mint. Or has the government mint run out of paper?

(The Cabinet is soaked in back-slapping self-congratulation. Finance's face is a register of surprise and disgust)

EXT. AFFAIRS: If I may come in at this point, it is really not wise to print more money at this moment, otherwise the supply of money will exceed the quantity of goods, and the result will be inflation *(sensing the blankness on the surrounding faces)* eh eh eh that is, goods becoming too expensive.

PUB. MORALITY: *(Her face screwed up)* Aaaa ... Àbí o ... This *oyinbo* is too much *jare*. *(Hitting on another new idea)* yes eh eh eh ... What about the Maize Fund?

AGRIC: O hoo! The six hundred million arina saved for the Maize Project.

HEAD: Oh! Oh! *O kare!* That reminds me. Why should we

chase to Sókótó what we have here in the pocket of our sòkòtò? ... Transfer half *(pause, hesitation)* Transfer the entire amount to the Welcome Project.

FINANCE: The entire six hundred million?

HEAD: Yes oo!

(The Cabinet registers a noisy approval)

FINANCE: *(His face aflame with protest)* But, but ...

AGRIC: *(Snapping in)* What is but there? It has happened before. Remember that the money for our Water Dam Project was diverted to the funeral of our leader's grandfather. Afterall, it was the people who ate the food and drank the wine.

FINANCE: But — but — but this is crazy. I have already told the nation about the Maize Project at a widely publicised press conference. And—

HEAD: Oh, is that the problem? What is *keresi* about that? We can always unsay what we have already said. Sergeant! *(Sergeant roundabout-turns, executes a ferocious salute)* Call in the journalist.

Journalist enters, a camera slung across his shoulders, carrying a sheaf of papers in his left hand, and an abnormally long pen in his right. He has two other pens stuck between his ears and his head. He is shaking like one possessed. He puts down the papers and the pen, readies his camera and begins to snap. The Head motions him to a halt while he brings out a large handkerchief, wipes his face elaborately, adjusts his belt, and brushes his medals. He then puts on his cap and commences a series of grotesque poses. He grins, guffaws, frowns, tilts his head to the left, then to the right, stands akimbo, hangs both arms up like a bird about to fly, and finally assumes a salute posture. The Journalist keeps on snapping; then turns to the Cabinet who are dying for him to record their own grotesque postures.

Agric rearranges the folds of his agbada, belches loudly, smiles broadly; External Affairs adjusts his cap, takes out his handkerchief wipes his face, smiles broadly; Public Morality whips out her compact, dabs her face, with a thick layer of powder, paints her lips ruby-red with an extraordinarily big lipstick, rises from her seat, adjusts her gele, rewraps her wrapper, stands chest out with her left hand in an akimbo position, her right under her chin, head slightly tilted backward, smiles broadly; Finance merely looks on.

The Journalist snaps and snaps, frantically rewinding his camera. He kneels, bends, lies prostrate, stands tip-toe, etc.

HEAD: Okay! *O too!* How many rolls of films have you used?

JOURNALIST: My Head, my Leader, my Lord, Lion of Yanke, only twenty rolls, twenty four shots each ...

HEAD: Making four hundred and eighty shots altogether, eh?

JOURNALIST: Yes, our God-chosen, our Messiah.

HEAD: That's not bad. I think we can now begin our discussion with him.

EXT. AFFAIRS: Yes, Journalist, pick up your pen and write.

(Journalist scurries back to his papers, picks up his jotter and pen and scribbles frantically as the Cabinet speak)

AGRIC: *Akòwé*, last week, Finance—

JOURNALIST: *(Looking lost, unsure)* Eem ... eem ...

AGRIC: Eeh, that man *(pointing)* eeeh ... Minister of Finance ... announced at a news conference that we have collected six hundred million arina for the Maize Project.

JOURNALIST: Yes, Sir, and I put it in the most conspicuous part of the *Daily Gist*, and I ...

AGRIC: Alright, alright. Write in your paper again that it is not true.

JOURNALIST: Ah! How ...?

EXT. AFFAIRS: OK, OK. Just say that you just had a frank and fruitful discussion with the Cabinet and discovered that the six hundred million arina announced by the Finance Minister last week for the Maize Project has, in fact, not been received. So, the Minister announced it *(hesitates)* by mistake ... e e ... in error ... Through oversight ... No, as a matter of fact, the Minister didn't actually say that. His statement was misconstrued ... He was misquoted ... *(Agric. and Pub. Morality exchange blank, confused looks).* Create a small but conspicuous column apologising for any embarrassment this might have caused the Cabinet ... eh ... eh the government.

FINANCE: But it was true ... I ... said it. And all the papers carried the news. So did the radio and television. How can I turn round to say I did not say what I actually said?

HEAD: I think I should come in here. *(All eyes turn to the Head, especially those of Finance, who looks rather expectantly. The Head wipes his face and belches loudly).* I am calling you to order, Finance. Ah ah, what is the problem? You said you said something and we are saying you did not say it. *Abi?*

EXT. AFFAIRS: Yes, yes, this is not the first time such things have happened. They are a regular occurrence in the process of governance. And protocol. In diplomatic circles, such denials are called *(with ostentatious emphasis)* restatements.

HEAD: Ahaaa! Thank you External. You are a true son of your father. I know you will find the right words for it. *(Becoming even more expansive).* You see, we have the power to say and unsay. We control the newspapers and the radio and television, and we can always tell them what to say. Afterall we spend a lot on these media and we must get our money's worth. The too-knows who shout for freedom of speech don't know what they are talking about. Some of them should still be sucking at their mothers' breasts.

EXT. AFFAIRS: My Head, the Lion of Yanke, I see no problem here. If they demand freedom of speech, we reserve the freedom of policy and action not to permit it. In diplomatic circles, that's what we call *tit-for-tat*.

HEAD: Alright Journalist, you hear? Put it in your paper. It is the first thing I will look for tomorrow morning.

AGRIC: And you know *akowe*, if you do this well, we always know how to reward you. When a child washes his hands clean, he will eat with elders. *(Facing the others) Abi? (Suddenly grabbing his stomach)* oh that word again! My Head, Lion of Yanke, where is our refreshment? My stomach is a battlefield for a thousand wolves. *Yeepa ebi deee* ...!

JOURNALIST: But ... but Lion of Yanke, the people will know. The ... the ... market women ... the students ... the ... the...

HEAD: Di di di what? Who are the people when we talk about government? What are they? By the Grace of God, we are the government today ... The people ... the people, well the people may do what they like. Afterall they didn't vote us into power, and we are never going to ask them for votes. God in His infinite wisdom has put this crown on our head ... *abi*? We are in power today!

ALL THE MINISTERS: *(In a strident chorus)* And all days!

HEAD: *(Happy, reassured)* Thank you. We have the people in our hand. We decide what they eat, where they sleep, when they live, when they die. We may banish them, dissolve them if we choose. Our government owes nothing, absolutely nothing to their existence. *(Laughs hysterically)* Yes ... and those students again! Why are you so scared of them? We are not *(facing the Cabinet) abi*? Just pluck a dozen *(snaps fingers)* from the crowd and the rest will not need to be told what to do. Maybe it is time for another lesson: those students are overstepping their bounds again. Instead of reading and writing and praying for their rulers, they take to the streets, shouting, carrying placards raining abuses on those of us who labour night and day to serve them.

EXT. AFFAIRS: My Head. Lion of Yanke, it is the Cubans.

ALL: The Cu...!

HEAD: *(Visibly shaken)* Kumbans ... eh?

AGRIC: *Yeee. Ori mi oo! Ibosi oo!*

EXT. AFFAIRS: Yes. In diplomatic circles, Cuba is known as the revolution expert of the world. Every goat, every sheep in Cuba knows Karl Marx. Nursery rhymes are spiced with the banners of Che Guevara. Even the leaves of Cuba's trees are red with rebellion. *(Noticing that his colleagues are absolutely lost, and coming down to simpler, more mundane things)* ... the Cubans are out to destroy the rich and turn over power to the poor. They hate the Mercedes like shit ... *(holding his nose)* ... oh pardon me for that undiplomatic language.

HEAD: But how did the students get to know Cuba and all those jaw-breaking people ... eh eh ... names you mentioned? One of the first progressive acts of this government was to ban all foreign ideologies, burn all Communist books, and impose heavy penalties on whoever tried to import them into our country.

AGRIC: Ah ah those Kumbans! I understand that they can make themselves invisible while they deposit their books by the millions on university shelves ... they also dissolve their ideology in the air so that our students can breathe it. Ah ah those Kumbans!

PUB. MORALITY: My Head, as our people say, a desperate problem needs a desperate solution. Instead of sitting here and shivering like women ... I mean ... like cowards, let us think of how to handle these students so that they don't ruin the good work our government is doing.

HEAD: Yes, thank you Morality. We shall tighten our security belt, recruit more spies among students and lecturers ... and send more of our own spies to the campus.

AGRIC: My Head, the Lion of Yanke, that may not do. The students know many of our spies among them. They even know how much we pay them. And in times of crisis, they always pounce on our eyes on campus as traitors. Remember they almost cut off the head of that our boy ... eh eh eh *(trying to remember the name)* Moik ... yes, Moik Uyee. Remember what they did to that black Citroen *(pronounced "Sitiron")* which we gave to him. My own suggestion is very simple: let us cut the supply of food to their campus every now and then. Growling stomachs will make them prostrate on their bellies.

PUB. MORALITY: I have another suggestion: since it is the men who make trouble all the time, let us ban female visitors from the campus. That will make them impotent ... I mean powerless.

AGRIC: Ah ah ah! No ooo! That is not good at all. The men will turn loose on their female counterparts. I have three daughters at Uniyanke, and I ...

PUB. MORALITY: Then build a maternity at the back of your house.
(General laughter)

HEAD: Alright, alright. I will mention this to the commander of the Garrison Organisation. We shall ask the police to keep greater watch. Let any of these students make *peke* and cross our path. They will enjoy the kindness that is our custom to extend to the opposition ... Let them try. They will know that the Lion on our immoral ... eh eh eh ...armorial bearing is not a lamb ... Journalist, now you can go. Remember all we said. *(As Journalist is about to exit)* And don't forget to add that everything is in the national interest.

JOURNALIST: Yes, Sir. Lion of Yanke, and for the peace and stability of our dear fatherland. *(Takes an agitated exit.)*

The group exchange congratulatory looks and breathe sighs of relief. But that momentary quiet is shattered by one of the guards who accidentally drops his rifle while trying to extricate a ferocious soldier ant from his underpants. He thrusts one hand into his groin area while helplessly scratching his right thigh with the other. The bang caused by the falling rifle throws the Cabinet into tantrums: the HEAD leaps off his chair and dashes for cover under the table; EXT. AFFAIRS makes for the door; while AGRIC and PUB MORALITY collapse on their knees, hands stretched forward in prayerful frenzy mumbling incoherently, one shouting "Jehofa!", the other "Allah!", sweating and shaking. FINANCE, who never rises from his seat, watches all the circus with perplexed equanimity ... After a long, anxious while, the HEAD, seemingly recovering his wits, bellows "Guard!" The Guard bellowing back "Yessso!" picks up his rifle and resumes his former position. "Normal" life gradually comes back to the group. EXT. AFFAIRS adjusts his cap (or tie if wearing a suit), AGRIC and PUB. MORALITY wipe their knees and sweaty faces, and adjust their robes. A feverish shake of the right leg indicates that the Guard is really not at ease ... A long, awkward pause, then the HEAD braves himself back to life.

HEAD: Sorry Gentlemen and Lady. Ah, that was something else! You see, soldiers have grown so soft these days. *(As if lost in thought)* Ah, when our country was still a colony, I used to stand at ease for several days in front of the Governor-General's residence. And what a good loyal soldier I was! I polished the officers' shoes till they shone like a mirror. My fame rapidly spread as the greatest shoe-polisher in the whole army, and soon I got the nickname "Pabo the Polishman". I carried out orders without looking back, obeyed without ever complaining.

I didn't pass many of the *"bukuru"* exams, but I got promotion for my hard work. Ah, those *oyinbo*, they all knew me and they gave me medals every Empire Day. And gradually, I rose through the ranks — and to the top. Those *oyinbo*, ah they helped me to the top, because they knew I polished shoes like no one else; they knew I was no troublemaker. Yes, that was how it started. Now I am a General. I command the army. I command the country ... Ah, those were good days. Soldiers were soldiers. No messing around with bloody civilians. These days you can hardly differentiate between soldiers and Boy Scouts. *(Suddenly coming out of his reverie and facing the group, he breaks into a peal of laughter.)*

AGRIC: *Abi o*? Thank God our Head, the Lion of Yanke, didn't read any of those fat books. If he had read them, if he had passed those exams, he would not have been the good, wise, and *(searching for the right word)* ... officious ruler he is today. Thank God for soldiers like you, and for your good and simplistic rule. Without you, who would have saved our dear country? *(A roar of approbation from the others except FINANCE)*

HEAD: Thank you, Agric ... Thank you all ... Eh heen, as I was saying, *(becoming really expansive)* you may be wondering how that journalist became so tame *(laughs)*. You see, for me and heroes like me, the easiest horse to train is the stubbornest one. Increase its dose of whips as well as its ration of food and it surrenders its back even before you ask for it. *(Pauses, paces up and down, full of swagger)* The journalist you have just seen was a really stubborn horse. His pen set the *Daily Gist* ablaze, and he was called the spitfire of Wawaka, the place where his pen daily spat venom like a cobra. *(Laughs)* But with a little threat here and there, and a lot of money and other sweet things, we removed that venom and turned the cobra into a harmless string, ready to bend wherever you wish. *(Laughs)* Not his fault. Afterall he is human: he is Yankean *(General shouts of approbation ... The Head now turning his head in another direction)*. Now, Finance, what is inside you that has kept you so silent since ...

AGRIC: Yes, I too have observed that he has said nothing for many minutes now. Heeen? What is your problem? You better talk now or we may mistake your silence for a conspiracy against our government.

PUB. MORALITY: True o. The man is just sitting there swollen like a ripe boil. Better speak out.

FINANCE: What is there to say when rulers have turned liars like prophets of the Bar Beach; when those pretending to be statesmen say one thing while they mean another? What am I to tell the poor people of Yanke? That their long and painful suffering and starvation have to continue because their Hunger Relief Funds have been diverted to the hosting spree of overfed dictators and their followers? Last year thousands of our countrymen and women perished: parents buried their own children; there were so many corpses that we didn't have enough hands to bury them. Our northern district was reduced to ribs and skulls. Hunger devastated our country like an epidemic. The entire world came to our aid and provided Maize Funds to see us through the present travail and secure us against future disasters. Last year was terrible, and this year is only a little better. Already ...

AGRIC: Oh oh oh! We know all this already. We were living witnesses to it all and ...

FINANCE: No, you were *(emphatically)* fattening witnesses to it all, and you know what I mean. *(Pause)* Anyway, as I was saying, already this year there has been a shortfall in the production of food as a result of the protracted drought. A cob of maize costs a fortune and soon there will be nothing left on the market. Unless the funds are spent judiciously, soon there will be hunger again, then death.

PUB. MORALITY: But tell me, Mr Too-know, how many of your own people died last year? If people know how to prepare for their own people, there will be no hunger. *(pause)* Afterall, bad as things seemed to be, Agric managed to feed his eight wives and sixty five children, and his bankers have not been complaining; External Affairs had enough for his family here and plenty to send to his concubines in Lisbon. Our friends in Switzerland have not had any cause to doubt our loyalty.

AGRIC: A haa! That is life. All of us cannot have enough to eat at the same time. But the rulers must be served first so that they can have enough strength to serve the people. You see, fingers are not equal. *(Gripping his stomach)* Oh those wolves again! When shall we have our refreshment?

EXT. AFFAIRS: Yes, I agree: fingers are not equal. Even in the USA and USSR, and other civilised countries, the people make their rulers comfortable. In diplomatic circles, that's what we call *(emphatically)* reasoned disparity.

FINANCE: The rulers, yes, must have enough strength to bury their subjects. But I will leave you to explain to the people how funds meant for relieving their hunger have gone into feeding state guests. I have suffered these contradictions long enough; now I find it difficult to live with myself and my conscience. Lion of Yanke, this is your portfolio!

He slams his file on the Head's table, grabs his briefcase and tears out of the room. At the exit point, one of the Guards springs into action and blocks his way. There is a slight scuffle. The Head shouts "Guard, give way!" The Guard complies, salutes briskly and freezes back into his former position.

AGRIC: My Head, why did yon do that? You should have

ordered him to shoot him directly. Now he is free to go and tell lies about us to the people. *Ori mi o!* We are playing with a revolution o!

EXT. AFFAIRS: No, the Head is right. If you kill him here and now, you turn him into a martyr and ...

AGRIC: I say kill him dead, not turn him into Martha, a mere woman!

EXT. AFFAIRS: I mean saint ... eh eh martyr means saint ...

AGRIC: Oh oh oh! The type they have in the Bible? *(But still looking blank.)*

EXT. AFFAIRS: Yes. We shall devise other means of doing away with him without appearing to have done so. *(With an air of self-importance)* In diplomatic circles, we call that sanitised elimination.

HEAD: *(Somewhat agitated)* I agree with you, External. That bastard has the boldness to challenge our authority. We shall tell him that it is not for nothing that ours is called The Land of the Prowling Lion. *(Pause)* This throne is ours and so shall it remain until we die and pass it on to our children and children's children. We are living in the era of life presidents and presidents-for-life, and we have to move with the times. As for me, I will not live to be called ex-president, ex-this, ex-that.

(A sharp blackout)

Act II

Frontage of an opulent 'Supermarket with large shop windows flaunting the latest in European fashion. And its most expensive too. There are gorgeously dressed female and male manikins with blond hair and blue eyes. One of the windows displays sports outfits ranging from track suits to tennis rackets and golf sticks; another is crowded with wigs of all shades of colour. Shoppers and loafers, carrying all kinds of shopping bags, can be seen making interminable exits and entrances.

A sharp solo rises offstage, achieving a crescendo as beggars enter the stage from the left, settling in front of the "Supermarket", a few metres from the shop windows.

A young woman in iro and buba with a baby on her back, throws a coin into the blind man's bowl before disappearing into the shop. The lucky receiver feels out his harvest, and proclaims to the other beggars' hearing, "Ah! It is one arina!" whereupon the lame breaks into a throaty song: "Owó to fuń wa" while the others chorus: "Jàgùdà ò ri já". They dance briefly, with Sule drumming on his bowl with the arina coin.

SULE: *(excitedly)* Today looks like a good day. There must be a rainbow in the sky.

OBI: *(looking up)* No such thing. Remember today is Monday, and we must reap the accumulated dues of the weekend.

SULE: O yes, sacrifices for a profitable week.

ETIM: Sacrifices for good luck, sacrifices for wealth.

OBI: Sacrifices for the twentieth wife, sacrifices for the seventieth child.

SULE: Sacrifices! Sacrifices! *(Pause)* Are we vultures or crows that we must live off the crossroads of fortune?

OBI: Not exactly, but we are victims of fortune at the mercy of a merciless world. Remember, nobody gives you anything unless they have been so instructed by their *dibia* or

Sometime last year, I was sitting under the bridge at our usual place near Koto. It was late evening. Suddenly I heard a truck pull up by the roadside, and about three men jumped down and pounced on me.

OBI: Mba, three men at a time?

ETIM: Then who is the father?

ABEKE: Ah ah, you just wait. *(Pause)* From their grip I knew they must have been young men in their twenties. The feel of their hands showed they had been handling something hard for a long time. Anyway, they grabbed me and bundled me into the waiting truck.

SULE: What did the other beggars do, our other colleagues?

ABEKE: What could the lame and the blind have done with thugs stronger than steel?

ETIM: You mean they just looked on while those apes dragged you away?

OBI: What could they have done?

ABEKE: Of course, they did something, something more symbolic than really effective. The lame swung free their arms and hauled stones and broken bricks at the truck; one of my blind friends used the only weapon he had — his stick. He threw it at the truck, it landed straight in it, and it sped away with it.

ETIM: The brutes! Depriving a blind man of his stick!

ABEKE: Yes, they did. Others who couldn't throw anything shouted curses and abuses at the kidnappers. *(Pause)* After a long drive, we came to a house. It must have been a very lonely place: there was so much silence all around. Silent as a funeral: no sound of laughter, no sound of mothers singing lullabies to rock their babies to sleep, no sound of singing birds. Only the clang of iron gates opening and closing.

OBI: Then what happened?

ABEKE: As the gates swung shut behind us, a rough voice came from inside the mansion: "Oh, is that her? Bring her in." The thugs pushed me into what must have been a large sitting room from the way our voices echoed and echoed.

OBI: Then what happened?

SULE & ETIM: Heeey, have patience now!

ABEKE: The man stood up and came close to me. He was breathing hard like one being pursued. "Ah, she is so beautiful," he said, coming closer still, "how did this one manage to be blind? OK, wash her up and bring her back to me" *(pause)*. So those brutes stripped me naked and, pretending to bathe me, took liberties with every part of my body, then took me upstairs to their master. *(Long pause)*

OBI: And ...

ABEKE: And what a terrible room that was: smelling so strongly of alcohol and other things. I felt like throwing up ... *(pause.)* The master came close again breathing hard. He must have been a really fat and heavy man. His breath was hot and seemed to choke the room. *(Pause)* First, he touched my hair. Then he put his hand on my shoulder, and I flung his hand away. He retreated, breathing heavily, waited for a while, before making for the loose end of the big towel in which his thugs had wrapped me. Before I knew what was happening his mouth dashed for my breasts, his breath reeking like a public latrine. I summoned all the strength in my little body and rammed my right knee into his big stomach. He fell back with a grunt, then shouted for his thugs to come. They rushed in, held me down while their master ... The result is the baby I hold in my hands. *(Starts sobbing)*

SULE: Just like that?

ABEKE: *(Responds with a nod.)*

ETIM: Has he come to see you since that time?

ABEKE: No. *(Goes into a state of semi-withdrawal, rocking her baby and singing silently to herself)*

OBI: But how could he have done that to you? What makes a rich man with many wives develop a terrible appetite for a helpless blind woman?

ETIM: Ah! I have never seen the like before.

SULE: I have. It often happens. He has done it to buy back his good luck.

OBI & ETIM: Good luck? How?

SULE: The jujuman often recommends it. When a man has been having a run of bad luck — failing business, failing relationships, no success with women, failing manhood, and so on — it is believed that a sexual act with a beggar will cure him.

OBI & ETIM: But how?

SULE: Haa haa haa! My friends there are many things you need to know about the way these big people think. They believe we are special people, that we can make things happen. Some even believe that a beggar's head placed in a platter in the dark corner of a room produces money by the millions. Some people will do anything to become rich, and the rich will do anything to remain so. *(Pause)* This is why our colleagues have been disappearing without trace.

ETIM: So we are victims in two ways

OBI: Victims in more ways than two

ETIM: Ashes in the fireplace of wealth

OBI: And the faggot consumed by the fire of money

ETIM: Forced out here that some may live in big mansions

OBI: Then carted off and turned into money-making mummies

in the dark corners of the millionaire's mansion.

ETIM: It must be true that money robs the rich of their senses.

OBI: It must be the deafening rustle of currency notes, the blinding glitter of gold.

SULE: *(Breaking in to change the topic)* By the way, I understand another state visit is on the way.

ETIM & OBI: A state visit?

OBI: Heey! How do you know?

SULE: It is sight I lack, not hearing. And when the eyes cannot see, the ears double their power. I have listened well and heard the footsteps of ants.

ETIM: OK, OK, what have the ants said this time?

SULE: The Leopard of Wilama, Father of the Nation, God-chosen, President-for-Life, is coming on a state visit...

OBI: Get bigger bowls, friends, bigger bowls! I understand the Wilama government is very, very, very generous to beggars: that is how the rulers bribe God for their crimes.

ETIM: Heey! Before you die dreaming, remember what happened when the Tiger of Goto came on a visit the other time. Remember how we were all carted off like pigs?

SULE: That's right. But we felt his presence. Wherever he went we knew because we recognised him by the jingling of his medals.

ETIM: Ah! Na waah o! The man went back richer: he received various presents, including two girls donated by an upcountry chief to increase the Tiger's harem.

(The beggars' lively exchange is interrupted by the entry of two hefty men carrying large buckets of paint and long brushes, their garments bespattered with the liquid of their trade. They are accompanied by an ill-fed, frail-looking policeman with a truncheon hanging from his oversize

shorts. The three burst in from stage right, strut up and down with an exaggerated sense of importance, then make straight for the beggars.)

POLICEMAN: Heey you people, what do you think you are doing littering this place and making this ugly noise? Move away from here before it is too late!

SULE: Why? What is all this shout about? We never thought we were sitting on anybody's head ...

(The other beggars nod in agreement)

POLICEMAN: Maybe not, but right now you are sitting on the head of the law. Something important is about to happen here. Our country is expecting a guest and this *(pointing)* being our main street, must be completely, thoroughly, mercilessly ... clean.

(The beggars exchange a kind of didn't-I-tell-you glance. A steel stubbornness is written on their faces)

SULE: Where do you want us to go?

POLICEMAN: Home, of course, home!

ETIM: We have no home

OBI: This is our home

ABEKE: *(Stirring from her apparent reverie)* Here and under the bridge, by the roadside, and in the marketplace.

ETIM: We live here

OBI: We eat here

ABEKE: *(Displaying her baby)* We breed here

OBI: We eat here

ETIM: We drink here

ABEKE: We starve here

OBI: We piss here

37

ETIM: We shit here

POLICEMAN: *(Holding his nose)* You are a disgrace to the nation, the dirt of our streets

SULE: *(Cutting in, and with a self-confidence which surprises the Policeman)* We are the conscience of the nation, the scruple of the streets

ABEKE: We are the problems you avoid in the day, which become your monsters at night

POLICEMAN: You squirm in the filth of unwashed bodies

SULE: Your bosses fester in unpunished crimes

POLICEMAN: You wretched lot! You tread the law in the face. Remember the law's patience is not inexhaustible.

SULE: You call us wretched? So we must be if your masters are to keep on riding fat cars and living in stolen mansions. Their tyres drench us in sewer water; that's why we are dirty; their greed ravages the land, that's why we are hungry.

ETIM: Why must we be swept into the sea because the Elephant of Wilama, or whatever he's called is coming? Doesn't he have beggars in his own country?

OBI: Of course, remember the big influx the other time, when Wilama beggars flooded our streets and drove us all out of job? Some of them were young, long-haired beautiful girls who walked straight into the middle of heavy traffic to ask motorists for alms. For some time, our rich lost their patriotism to these invading beauties.

SULE: We beggars must unite against these injustices. Just consider this: the rich steal your food and then punish you for being hungry. Our rulers cast us on the streets and then jail us for homelessness ...

ABEKE: Tell us, *Oga poliisi*, do you think it is our wish to be here, scorched by the sun, beaten by the rain, spat upon by people, carted away to make juju? *(Moving closer to the policeman, while the latter begins to back away)* Look at your stomach. *Oga poliisi,* does it look like those of your masters?

SULE: *(Somewhat pensively)* Yes, we should unite — all the beggars in this country. I understand that in Ganisel, a country just a few miles from us, beggars have a trade union ...

(The other beggars are excited at this idea, and demonstrate it in their reactions. The Policeman, obviously out of patience, becomes agitated and begins to shout. He wields his truncheon, stands at attention, assumes the salute posture, all like one in a state of incipient dementia.)

POLICEMAN: Aalllllrightl Move! Enough is enough! You have exhausted the patience of the law. I say Moooovel *(Begins to blow his whistle frantically. To the Policeman's surprise, instead of moving away, the beggars move closer together, laughing and taunting the agent of the law. He swears, curses, and fumes even as the beggars break into song. The Beggars' Anthem should also be boldly printed and displayed frontstage for clear reading by the audience):*

We are the rags by the long roadside
Who challenge the pompous wardrobe
For them who have a lot to hide
We are the thorn, the forgotten probe

Hard as stone, loose as dust
Held together by a league of lice
Cast of steel that will never rust
We outlast the King and his glittering lies

In shine, in cloud, in pouring rain
Huddled and bundled, we defy the skies
In every joint an aching pain
A feast for bugs and famished flies

> Crawling, staggering, feeling our way
> We're the nation's pulse, its handicap
> Hidden at night, we are out by day
> The broken feather on the nation's cap

POLICEMAN: *(Carried away, then gathering himself together)* Eeee! I pity you! You are toying with the sharp edge of the law, and it cuts ...

SULE: Cuts, cuts, cuts ... Yes, we know. Like the butcher's knife, it cuts through the flesh and falls shy of the bones. We *(pointing to his colleagues)* are the soft, crumbling flesh: the rich and powerful are the bones.

ABEKE: They make laws

ETIM: And break them

POLICEMAN: *(Trying to laugh derisively)* Can't you see how powerless you are before the onslaught of the Law? See, some of you are blind: others don't have legs to stand upon. *(Laughs again)*

SULE: We are made of something the law can never conquer

OBI: We are the dust of the earth

ETIM: The blue of a sunny sky

ABEKE: The seamless womb of the earth

SULE: The waters of the oceans

ETIM: And shells worn smooth and hard by the waves

OBI: The cat's eye that defies the dark

ETIM: The rags that outlive the robe

POLICEMAN: *(His impatience returning. Stamps the ground with his right foot)* Now this has to stop! Can't you see we must not wash our dirty linen in the street?

SULE: Yes, we must stuff them in the inner rooms and choke from the smell

ETIM: Or wash them at night and throw the water in our neighbour's frontyard

OBI: Or wear stolen clothes daily and pretend we never sweat

ABEKE: Or jail those who say the country smells ...

(The Policeman has had enough. He stands at attention once again, executes a brief salute, blows his whistle several times, hurls up his truncheon, and charges at the beggars who scurry offstage, the Policeman in hot pursuit. The Painters, suddenly bursting out of their frozen state like robots, dip their brushes into their buckets and start splashing white paint all around. Sharp blackout.)

Act III

Another Cabinet meeting. This time, the Head is dressed like a civilian — in flowing agbada with a cap to match. The Cabinet is seated as usual, and its mood appears more upbeat than before. A new Minister of Finance is now in place, a vain, obsequious replacement. The two entrances are guarded as usual by stern-looking soldiers, but this time, the Head's bodyguard is a heavily built policeman in para-military uniform, who stands rather diffidently behind his throne-like chair. The lights come gradually on as the Cabinet commences action, beginning with the national anthem.

HEAD: Welcome again. Lady and Gentlemen. Let me start by specially welcoming our new Minister of Finance. *(Finance rises from his seat with an exaggerated sense of self-importance.)* We are happy to see you here. As you yourself will soon see, we are a good government ruling over very ungrateful people. Heeh? So many detractors! But we know that no government can be doing all the good things we are doing without having enemies from inside and outside *(Shouts of agreement from the Cabinet)*. But play your part well, and I promise you — you and your family, your friends and all those lucky enough to be your relations will never know poverty for ever.

(Laughing sheepishly and bowing several times, his cap or hat in his hand, Finance sinks ostentatiously back in his seat, his colleagues cheering loudly.)

AGRIC: Aaah! *Akiika!* True word! Just obey our Head, cooperate with us, and there will be plenty for you to eat. *(Pause)* Heen, which reminds me, has anybody made arrangements for our refreshment?

PUB. MORALITY: Haah! Agric *(Slapping him on the thigh)* you and food: one will kill the other! The meeting has not even started, and you are already dying to eat!

AGRIC: *(Feigning anger)* My Head, warn this woman oo! Just see where she hit me *(demonstrating)*, dangerous place! Aaah! Too close to the powerhouse!

HEAD: *(Joining indulgently in the irresponsible joke)* Haaa! Public Morality, you must be careful where you hit a man oo. Especially an active man like Agric! *(A general oblivious laughter. Pause)* Yes, as I was saying ... or was about to say, the day of the visit is drawing nearer and nearer. I have called this meeting to discuss how far we have gone with the preparations. *(The Cabinet nods in agreement)* As our people say, when a man's eyes are small, he starts weeping from a distance when invited to a funeral. *(Another roar of approbation, with Agric shouting "Ẹ ṣé Bàbá, ẹ́ẹ́ pà mirlin!...)* Now Public Morality, how far have you gone?

PUB. MORALITY: *(Adjusting her 'gele')* My Head, Saviour of Yanke, the only lion that husbands a whole herd *(half-kneeling)* all honor, all glory to you. *(Pause)* Our people are really ready for this visit. Everywhere I go, the faces I meet are full of expectation. All the Boys and Girls Clubs have been told to select the best of their dancers for the airport show — agile young boys and beautiful girls *(demonstrating)* with breasts erect and firm.

AGRIC: *(Wriggling in his seat)* Aaah! *Ina pitii!* Sure fire! *Akiika!*

HEAD: Eeee, what about the Press?

AGRIC: The Press? But the *Daily Gist* has already promised to cooperate.

FINANCE: Yes, but that's not the only one around.

PUB. MORALITY: Alright, no alarm, I have spoken to all and I have them all here *(pointing to a closed fist)*. They have promised not to publish anything the Head would not like to hear ...

FINANCE: *(Apprehensively)* What about *The Telling Tempo*?

AGRIC: That's right o! Ah, those fire eaters of Ijake! Only God knows what is wrong with those boys. They don't want to eat like the others. You try to befriend them, it is impossible! You send them gifts, they throw the things back at your face ... Aaah! We put them in jail, burn their press, their terrible papers still keep coming out! Those boys must have plenty of *juju*. They say witches and invisible spirits print their papers for them in the night! Aaah!

FINANCE: My Head, those boys are terrible. We must do something about them.

HEAD: *(Rattled, but trying to keep a straight face)* Eeeeh, don't worry. I will do something about them ... *(Pause)* Now, Public Morality, what else have you done?

PUB. MORALITY: Thank you, my Head. To prevent any accident, I have set up the Committee of Public Purity which will cooperate with the Head's Committee of Invisible Censors to make sure that things work the way we want.

EXT. AFFAIRS: A jolly thing to do. A jolly thing indeed. You see, news is like a commercial commodity: government has the right to ban it, restrict it, or place it under license. In diplomatic circles, that's what we call "information squeeze" which is part of the legitimate intelligence control of any nation.

AGRIC: *(Visibly flabbergasted)* Aaah! *Akiika! Iwin inú ìwé!* Book wizard!

FINANCE: *(Shaking his head)* Ah, External is a blessing to this government!

PUB. MORALITY: A special cloth is ready with pictures of you and the visiting Head printed on it. It will be made compulsory for all schoolboys and girls in the land.

HEAD: Which of my pictures did you use? I hope it is not the one the *Daily Parrot* likes using, the one in which my shoulders hunch forward like those of a leaping frog?

AGRIC & FINANCE: *(Scandalised,)* Aaaah! *Ó tì ò!*

HEAD: If it is that one, burn the clothes and throw the ashes in the sea.

(The Cabinet break into hysterical laughter)

PUB. MORALITY: They dare not! They used the one you took last National Day, with your radiant smile and gallant look.

HEAD: *O kare!* Good of you!

EXT. AFFAIRS: There is a small but important matter that I want us to settle *(pause)*. What arrangements have been, or are being made to provide sleeping partners for our visitor?

AGRIC: Aaah, sleeping partners? Is he not coming with his wives?

EXT. AFFAIRS: No.

HEAD: Agric, there are many things you can't understand unless you are a Head of State.

EXT. AFFAIRS: Providing such minimal comfort is quite legitimate in international protocol *(pause)*, at least in these parts of the world. It is one of our legacies from the Turks.

HEAD: Yes. I agree. That reminds me: about four years ago, the Independence Celebration of Toloze was almost ruined when two of the invited Heads of State hurried back home ...

FINANCE: Because they were not provided with sleeping partners?

HEAD: No, because the girls were not beautiful enough. One of the Heads said it was a national disgrace to insult him with an owl!

PUB. MORALITY: Aaaah! Such a disgrace can never happen

here. *(Boastfully)* We have more than enough girls here to satisfy a million Heads of State. By the time our girls are done with them, those men will hardly be able to stand upright.

(General laughter)

AGRIC: Aaaah! It must be a great pleasure *(pronounced pleyo)* to be a Head of State. Aaaah!

HEAD: Now let us talk to those appointed for special duties for the visit so we can know how far they have gone. Eeeee, you, call in the professor!

The Guard salutes briskly and dashes off-stage, returning seconds later with Professor. Professor appears in an outlandish, obviously uncomfortable three-piece suit; an oversized black academic gown whose tail sweeps the floor behind him, giving him the look of an old penguin; and round-rimmed Victorian spectacles. He carries a voluminous book and a sheaf of papers in one hand, leaving the other free to manipulate his mortar board. Fawning and irritatingly spineless, he walks with a high-shouldered stoop and speaks in an affected "Oxford accent". He bows very low as he enters and does so several times during his speech, finding it difficult to maintain eye contact with the Cabinet. Throughout, Professor's behaviour oscillates between a trembling helplessness and a swaggering, somewhat insane flourish.

HEAD: Eeee, Professor, welcome. I asked people to bring you so that you can tell us how far you have gone with the welcome address.

PROFESSOR: *(Bowing till his head nearly touches his toes)* Yes, Sir, the Head, the one and only Lion of Yanke. Em em em, actually, I am halfway through it. Em em ...

AGRIC: *(Cutting in)* Haaa, haa! You still have not finished? You started about two months ago!

EXT. AFFAIRS: If I may come in here, yes it takes much longer to write a good *(emphasis on "goood")* welcome address.

FINANCE: And an interesting one too — containing all the things that people would like to hear. *(Pause)* I learnt that about a year ago, the welcome address by the Leopard of Ireza was so dull that the visiting Head of State fell asleep.

EXT. AFFAIRS: Ooooh yes, I remember pretty well. The microphone picked up the snore and sprrrreeaaad it among the crowd.

PUB. MORALITY: Ṣíọ̀ọ̀! And what happened to the unfortunate writer of that speech?

EXT. AFFAIRS: He was instantly arrested and put in a dungeon where he could enjoy an uninterrupted sleep for the rest of his life!

General laughter with Agric and Pub. Morality hitting each other in "dangerous" places again, and each yelling at the other. Professor rearranges his gown, touches his mortar board, adjusts his glasses, shuffles his feet, his face wrinkled with apprehension.

HEAD: We are lucky in this country; there are many learned men ready—

PUB. MORALITY: And women! *(General laughter)*

HEAD: Ooooh! Yes, and women — who are always ready to serve this great nation — Yes, Kpofeso, when will you finish?

PROFESSOR: My Head, Your Majesty, Your Excellency ... em em em actually I would have finished but for the research involved. I ...

AGRIC: Research? What are you researching? Only a welcome address, and ...

FINANCE: I am surprised too. What kind of search are you researching?

PROFESSOR: Excuse me em em em. But I want this to be a *non pareil* ...

AGRIC: Hun un *Pari pa kinnin*?

PROFESSOR: *(Noticing his audience is in trouble)* I mean em em em one that has no equal, such as befitting our great nation and its great ruler. For the past few weeks I have been fasting, working, meditating, trying to dig up the major speeches of Napoleon Bonaparte, Otto von Bismarck, Benito Mussolini, Emperor Bokassa, Adolf Hitler, and other memorable figures whose speeches set the world on action. You are a great ruler, Your Excellency, and great words must come from great mouths. *(The Head nods)*

AGRIC: *Akiika!* Son of his father!

PROFESSOR: Your Excellency ... em em ... like how long would you like this speech to be?

The Head looks blank; turns to Ext. Affairs for rescue)

EXT. AFFAIRS: Yes ... we said the last two were too short. Well, make this one three hours ... yes, one hundred and eighty minutes ... that meets the international standard.

Professor gathers himself together, executes another awkward bow and makes for the exit; stops short just before the door, the Guard quickly looking in his direction; then turns diffidently back towards the Cabinet whose members look expectantly on.

PROFESSOR: *(After much difficulty making himself clear)* Em em em ... Your Excellency, eh eh em em ...

HEAD: Yes, I have not forgotten. *(Turning to the Cabinet)* He is talking about the vacant post of principal of our university college. *(Turning back to Professor)* I am looking into it. Right? You can go now. *(Professor shuffles his feet, but does not leave.)*

EXT. AFFAIRS: I think Professor is a very loyal citizen and deserves whatever honour our government can bestow ...

FINANCE: *(Cutting in)* And obedient too! And very respectful! I like the way he bows.

AGRIC: Yes, he is not like those other too-know troublemakers who are so proud because they know book ... *(Hissing loudly)* Abi na book I go chop? Hun un! *(Another hiss. The Cabinet breaks into a loud, derisive laughter.)*

HEAD: Alright, alright. You will hear from me after the visit.

PROFESSOR: Thank you, Your Excellency. I am most obliged ... I am most obliged. *(Exits bowing.)*

HEAD: *(To Guard)* Call in the next person.

The Guard re-enters with a heavily built man carrying something which looks like a bundle of cloth, then returns to his position.

HEAD: *(With a sense of pride)* Lady and Gentlemen, my new Medalsmith! *(Medalsmith bows mechanically)* Now, how far have you gone?

The Medalsmith bows again, elaborately unfolds the giant bundle in his hand, spreading it out first to the Cabinet, then to the audience: an imperial ceremonial coat bedecked with medals of different shapes, sizes, and colours, from top to bottom; dazzling in its gaudiness. The coat is so weighted down with decorations that the Medalsmith finds it difficult to hold it aloft for any length of time. A mixture of surprise and admiration holds the Cabinet hostage to silence. An excited exchange of glances, with PUB. MORALITY in particular holding her head in both hands, while AGRIC explodes a long and sharp whistle.

HEAD: *(Breaking the silence)* Lady and Gentlemen, that is our Coat, the garment of our nation, decorated with the best of our land's minerals. What do you have to say about it?

(*Pause*) Eh eh eh ... External, you are our eye on the world: is this good enough?

EXT. AFFAIRS: Not quite, my Head. (*The Cabinet express surprise*) We are living in an age of pomp and pageantry, when a nation's wealth and worth are measured by the state and quality of its ruler's apparel, the weight of the crown of its King or Queen, the demonstrated opulence of its Princes and Princesses. Sartorial pomp has a place in international parade, Your Excellency, and we cannot afford to lose our place in the vanguard of progressive nations.

FINANCE: I agree, External. We judge a nation by the crown of its ruler. It is a widely accepted fact that a ruler is nothing without his medals. Look at Britain; they put the best of their diamonds on their monarch's crown: Napoleon's crown was not only made of the rarest French minerals; at his coronation he placed the crown on his own head! So ...

AGRIC: It is true oo ... I hear that in Ireza, every horse in the imperial stable wears a necklace of gold!

PUB. MORALITY: Sọhpọhnọ o! And the women? They must have an entire hall full of jewels!

EXT. AFFAIRS: As I was saying, my Head, we must be prepared. The visiting Head is reputed for his extraordinary love of medals. Our great Ruler must not be outdone in this very important regard. We must protect our national pride.

HEAD: (*Accepting the challenge with a life-or-death determination*) Thank you, External! I will always be grateful to you for preventing an imminent disgrace. (*To Medalsmith*) Awe, cover every available space with medals — big, small, black, white, yellow, red, blue, brown, green ... Do not leave anything to chance! Make sure this decoration beats anything this country ... the world ... has ever seen. If possible, put medals on the sleeves and the trousers as well!

The Medalsmith clumsily folds up his charge, performs another mechanical bow, and exits. The Head looks in the direction of the Guard, snaps his fingers, and the Guard disappears, returning seconds later with three men. Two of these are soldiers, the third the Painter, a frail-looking man with shaggy hair and beard matted with paint. The two soldiers drag him in, booting him ferociously, a violation whose brutality increases as they come in full view of the Head. The Cabinet watches with a combination of interest and surprise. The Head motions a halt, whereupon the soldiers salute briskly, then stand at attention behind the Painter. Throughout the unfolding episode, the Painter's behaviour is marked by a mixture of anger and defiance.

HEAD: Are you the one that disobeyed our orders?

PAINTER: I am not a public painter: my brush wrinkles the face of tyrants.

THE CABINET: *(Profoundly scandalised)* Aaah!

HEAD: Just wait, Lady and Gentlemen. Let us hear him well. *(To Painter)* So you refused to paint the picture of me and my visiting friend — the picture we are to put in the market-square?

PAINTER: The brush has a pulse which only responds to the feelings of humans; monsters need a witch's broom for their self-image.

HEAD: *(The message lost on him)* Why did you not ask for money when you knew you did not have money for a brush, eeh? I know you people are poor *(laughs)* ... worshippers of the God of Penury. *(Pause)* I am ready to give you whatever you demand for this work. People tell me you have the straightest hand in the whole country and that your image is as perfect as nature's own *(Pause)* This is your chance to make money and walk in the fold of the powerful. *(Pause)* Look at what happened to Gbegidenu the sculptor. Until he did that huge statue of me which stands in front of the General Post Office, he was so poor he could hardly feed his wife and two children. Now he lives in a mansion in a quiet part of town and his children romp about in wealth. Why ...

PAINTER: *(Snapping in)* My wealth is the rainbow of creation; paint is the blood that flows in the veins of my stroke. That blood congeals in the arteries of the tyrant, and the heart of creation explodes with falseclap.

HEAD: Eeeh? *(Looks at the Cabinet who are mute with surprise. Only External seems to know what is going on, but he appears too bewildered to talk.)*

PAINTER: The rainbow atrophies, narrows to red on the canvas of oppression; water turns acid and burns the socket of the consciencide.

AGRIC: *(Crashing through his stupor)* Haah! What is all this rainbow talk about? We have brought you here to make money ... to eat ... to be rich, not to dream. *(Turning to the Head)* My Head, is this man normal?

HEAD: Eeh ... eeh ... They say a little bit of madness helps their trade ... maybe it is hallucination ...

PAINTER: A hallucination that fathers reality at its grimmest. A reality of skulls shattered under iron heels, of hunger baring ribs, deepening sockets, bloating bellies ... of parents burying children lost to avoidable plagues ... of rulers goose-stepping on a red carpet of blood ... of emperors sucking the blood of their subjects like vampires of the night ... of torture chambers and strange disappearances ... of human limbs stoking the fire of greed and gore ... *(Pause)* These are the realities of which my hallucination is made.

HEAD: *(Getting worried)* Haah haah ... We have not brought you here to talk like an oracle of doom. The question is very simple: will you or will you not paint our picture? One answer opens the way to abundant wealth, the other death.

As the Painter incants the following lines, the Head, apparently mesmerised, assumes the various physical postures "painted" by the words. It takes quite a while before the Head jerks back into consciousness. Thereafter he becomes angry and bloodthirsty.

PAINTER: There is no grace in your glitter, no wisdom in your "ways". To do your bidding, my brush would be coarser than the despot's moustache, its glide arrested in canvas-pit. A wobbled figure of a hell ogre, its tongue jutting out of its anus, teeth wild like a hyena's, neck long like a scarecrow's, nails long like a vulture's, eyes at the back of head, feet splayed backward, shoulders sprouting cobras in place of arms ...

HEAD: *(Trying to "come back", sweating)* What ... what ... is em em em ... is that your answer?

PAINTER: My hand stays rigid from powerbark, my brush stiff, my paint congealed. *(Pause, then with stunning emphasis)* I cannot permanence tyranny on my canvas.

AGRIC: *(Now furious)* A thousand logs of wood in your mouth, you son of a nonentity! How dare you bandy words with our Head, the Lion of our Land? Are you mad?

FINANCE: *Agbagaa! Eewo!* What is this?

PUB. MORALITY: Nobody ever does this and keeps his head on his neck afterwards. You have violated your allegiance to your leader, and that is treason.

PAINTER: *(Charging at the Cabinet, going from one to the other as he speaks, with the Head now edged to a corner, watching, mouth agape)* My allegiance is not to those who order massacres and bathe their lust in blood; not to them who eat the poor for lunch and their children for supper: not to bloated despots maggoting in the decay of affluence. My allegiance is to *Truth,* balm of conscience, one straight path through the universe, enemy of the serpent of deceit. *(Turning to the audience)* My allegiance is to the suffering legion with no roofs over their heads and no food in their stomachs. My allegiance is to those lean bones which fatten the paunch of the rich.

HEAD: *(Furious, a little strange)* Oh hell with a million fires! Oh whirlwind! Oh curses from the mouth of night! *(Pause)* Strange times! The Lion has allowed this rat's menace for too long. But as if a joke, the hunter's apron is becoming a permanent robe ... *(Becoming almost demonic, rushing towards the Painter as if preparing to attack him)* Who are you? You one-penny bread, you leftover from the leopard's meal, you rag for trampling horses, you dwarf without testicles, you toadstool, you hunchback, you gun without trigger, you nose without face, you lion with no claws, you ... you ... you ... *(Pause, looking stranger still, struggling to recover himself though still talking in a wild stentorian pitch)* Yes, yes who are you? Everyone here — every one *(pointing to his Cabinet)* is a descendant of either a chief or a warrior, with the noble blood running loudly in their veins. *(As if regaining some of his wit and swagger)* History and tradition have made us rulers of this land. How dare you stand here, son of a wretch, and call us names? You have opened your mouth wide; *(demonstrating)* we shall widen it till it reaches your ears. *(To the soldiers who brought the Painter)* Take him to Chamber 40 and *(throwing a thick, long noose at the soldiers)* let him know what it means to be the victim of our wrath.

SOLDIERS: Yes Saaaa!

(No easy task getting the Painter off the stage; he engages the soldiers in an epic struggle, nailing the Head and his Cabinet with a final indictment)

PAINTER: You murderer of the body, can you ever kill the spirit? You are a passing cloud. After you the rainbow shall come, and Earth's children shall see the light again. Shall see the light again. Shall see the light again. The children of light shall see the l-i-g-h-t a-g-a-i-n! *(His voice echoes and reverberates from outside and beyond the stage.)*

HEAD: *(Still dazed, sweating)* Wonder of wonders! I have never seen anything like this in my thirty years as Head of Yanke. Such foolishness! Aaah! What is the world turning to?

AGRIC: *(Prostrating)* Please my Head. Don't be annoyed. I think the boy is mad.

PUB. MORALITY: *(Holding out both hands as if in supplication)* My Head, please forgive us. Let them hang the boy seven times and throw his flesh to the dogs ...

EXT. AFFAIRS: *(Clearing his throat, speaking almost clinically)* Agric is probably right. It is a part of the madness of our times. If you investigate properly you will discover that the Painter is a Communist under heavy influence from Moscow or Beijing. It doesn't matter that he has never travelled abroad before. In diplomatic circles, that is called indoctrination by telepathy.

FINANCE: He must surely be a Communist: consider the number of times he mentioned "red"!

HEAD: Let him be as red as he can be in Chamber 40. Dead mouths do not argue. *(Now back to business)* Eeeh ... eeh ... Agric, have you consulted the Rain-maker?

AGRIC: Yes, my Head. This time he is taking five million arina to keep the skies quiet for three days. *(The other Ministers open their mouths in amazement at the cost, but none utters a word.)*

HEAD: Let him have anything as long as he does the job. What about the religious organisations?

PUB. MORALITY: Yes, my Head, I spoke to the Archbishop of

Yanke and the Chief Imam of Yanke. They have promised interdenominational prayers on Friday and Sunday. They have assured us that the Almighty is behind this great government and its God-fearing Head. No cause for alarm. They are praying for the success of the visit. God is on our side.

FINANCE: And traffic?

PUB. MORALITY: Colonel Anapa is taking care of that. I am sure he is around to tell us his progress.

HEAD: *(To one of the Guards)* Call in Colonel Anapa.

Colonel Anapa enters with two men in tow, one carrying a huge bundle of "koboko" (leather whips), the other a bundle of "atorin" (whips). The Colonel carries his swagger stick in one hand and a long whip in the other. He salutes briskly, then beckons to the carriers to set down their burdens.

AGRIC: *Akiika! Eeegun!* There is plenty here for stubbornness to feed upon.

EXT. AFFAIRS: But ... eh ... eh what are we doing with all this? Are we also performing the Ìjọ̀pá ceremony for the visiting Head of State?

PUB. MORALITY: *(Laughing demurely)* Your are a funny person, External. You have been too long in foreign capitals to know what *(pointing)* these do for the stubborn driver.

EXT. AFFAIRS: *(Turning his gaze to Colonel)* You mean eeh ... eeh ... flog drivers?

COLONEL: Yes, Sir. The most reckless, the most inconsiderate, the most selfish drivers in the whole world live in this country.

FINANCE: *(Scoffing)* External will not understand ... Many of those who sit behind the wheels in this country are beasts, wild beasts. Even our Head, the Lion of Yanke can testify to that. Not long ago, one wild beast of a driver ran into his entourage and killed about four people.

EXT. AFFAIRS: Then why not take them to court instead of whipping them? That way you discourage traffic offences by actually enriching the state through the fines they pay. In diplomatic circles, that is what we call indirect revenue accumulation through penal imposition.

COLONEL: We have tried that and failed, sir. The drivers know the right hands to place bribes, and before you know where you are, they are back on the roads and ready to speed and kill.

EXT. AFFAIRS: And so these?

PUB. MORALITY: Eee hen?

COLONEL: You can't imagine the wonders these have performed, sir ... Oh! Their judgment is fast and immediate: no come-today-come-tomorrow of the court house. *(Drags out one of the whip carriers, gets him prostrate as he demonstrates by actually whipping his buttocks).* A motorist offends, you grab him by the collar, drag him out of his vehicle, lie him face-down by the roadside, and put six solid strokes of this on his stupid back wai, wai, wai, fai fai fai ... Next time you won't need to tell him before he behaves.

(General laughter)

AGRIC: Haah! *Akiika!* It is what we call one-two business ... *(laughing again, his hands groping towards Pub. Morality's danger zone.)*

PUB. MORALITY: *(Pushing off Agric with a loud hiss)* Yes, even many of the motorists have written to the Traffic Offence Unit to say they like the instant judgment of this government. Many of them say it is a good test of their manhood.

COLONEL: Sir, to ensure the success of the coming visit,

soldiers, policemen, traffic wardens, etc. will wield the whip and keep the roads free. You can't believe it: the mere sight of a whip makes an obedient child of the most stubborn Yankean driver. They will respect nothing else.

Their demonstration done, Colonel executes a loud salute, and he and the Whip-carriers freeze in a corner.

HEAD: Thank you, my people, for your patience and understanding. With assets like you around me. I can boast that I have the wisest, truest, most thoughtful and most corruptible — eh ... eh ... incorruptible Cabinet in Africa. No wonder our great nation has gone from strength to strength, from greatness to greatness. Another test of this greatness is the coming visit. *(As he prays, the Cabinet, in a mock-divine pose, chorus "Ase!")* All the gods of the land will be with us; all our ancestors will stand behind us so that we will not fail in giving this great son of Africa the honour he so richly deserves.

(Black out)

Act IV

Open street or arena; a motley crowd throngs on stage from all directions (including the auditorium); workers, students, market women, beggars, the young, the old, and the aged; displaying different placards, some well-lettered and fancy, others merely but legibly scrawled: GIVE US FOOD, NOT WHIPS; WHERE HAS THE MAIZE FUND GONE?; MONKEY DEY WORK, BABOON DEY CHOP; WHERE ARE OUR DISAPPEARED COMRADES?; DOWN WITH THE SECRET POLICE; DOWN WITH DICTATORSHIP!; WE ARE ALL BORN EQUAL; BURN THE LION'S CLAWS! BURN, BURN!; then they burst into song:

> We build the house for all to live
> They cast us out into the street
> We kill the beast with our tiny stones
> They eat and throw us bones
>
> We build the house with sweat and pains
> They fill our lives with chains
> So join your hands, kill the Lion
> Burn evil with hot iron

Great tumult; then a wiry old man comes stage-front, leaning on a walking stick; the crowd makes way for him, treats him reverentially, gives him physical prominence.

OLDMAN: Thank you my people, for giving me a place to stand. May you all die with grey hair on your heads. *(The crowd responds.)* But these days that prayer hardly finds an answer. These days when those alive in the morning are never sure that police bullets will allow them to see the sun setting behind the trees.

  As our people say, when the leaves of a tree suddenly turn yellow, there must be some powerful evil at work beneath the earth. When an owl hoots at noon and the cock joins the chorus, does one need special eyes to see evil in the sky?

There is an owl in this land; and it has hooted for thirty years, forcing the sun of many of our youth to set at noon. *(Emphatically)* This land reeks with the suffocating stench of a lion which hungers for its own brood. *(Pause, audience reacts)*

The oldest of my children used to be the manager of the Central Bank, an honest straight-going person whose blood boiled at the sight of evil. *(Pause)* One day he went to work and never came back. The government said that his car jumped into a river, but you and I know that he was killed for not helping to protect the secret accounts of the Lion of Yanke in foreign banks.

Let me not make my own grief the centre of everybody's concern. There are hundreds in this country whose relatives have disappeared without trace. *(The crowd responds in agreement)*

Next planting season I will be eighty on earth ... and in this land. Never before has injustice been so rife; never have some people found it so easy, so profitable, to collaborate with evil, never have so few had so much and so many so little.

I am old now and can almost count the rest of my days on earth. The future is yours: what will you do with it? *(The crowd is stung; reacts)*

STUDENT: Permit my small shrill whisper after the deep thoughtful thunder of Papa. I speak for the students of Yanke, the traditional victims of the Lion and his cubs, the police ...

When we cry against injustice, when we demand that the present autocratic, backward-looking regime needs a drastic uprooting they say we are "*angry young men*". But tell me, isn't there a lot to be angry about in this land today? *(A loud y-e-s!)*

Buffoons mismanage our lives — rich fat buffoons,

pillars of the Swiss Bank, jackals of transnational companies, emergency contractors, "importers, exporters, and manufacturer's representatives", collaborating with foreigners to mortgage our future *(turning to the audience)*, yours and mine!

I tell you, they are rich because we are poor. And for them to remain rich, we must remain poor! *(Shouts of "No way!" "O ti ooo!")*

Down with "natives" who collude with foreign vultures to eat our flesh. Down with those whose wealth beggars the rest of humanity. Down with those who see starvation and pass it off as abstinence, and who tell the poor to eat grass like the cows of the field. Down with those who muzzle the voice of dissent and turn journalists into megaphones of official deceit. Down with builders of torture chambers and artisans of death.

(The crowd is moved, agitated; pressure building up)

WORKER: I speak for the workers of Yanke, the hands that turn the wheels and fix the bolts, the hands that till the land, bringing forth the best there is in the womb of earth. For many years now, the harder we have toiled, the poorer we have become. The rich have jerked up prices and our wages have melted in our pockets. Landlords triple rents overnight, and dangle ejection warrants like talismans. School fees are out of reach, so our children roam the streets. Hospital fees are beyond our means, so the sick die "peacefully" at home. The factories we work are owned by those unknown to us: the profit we generate finds its way abroad. They fire us at will, most times without a reason, and ...

1ST VOICE FROM THE CROWD: *(Preferably from the auditorium)* Action ... Action NOW!

WORKER: At this point I am sure you will like to know what happened to the Maize Fund. *(The crowd's face becomes a mask of expectation; a brief pause, then continues)* That money has been diverted to the Welcome Project and ...

2ND VOICE FROM THE AUDITORIUM: What? Welcome what?

WORKER: Welcome Project, I said. The whole six hundred million arina!

3RD VOICE FROM THE AUDITORIUM: You mean that money put there to save us from starvation? *O ti oo!* Tell me it is *not* true!

WORKER: Unfortunately it is. The entire thing will be spent on the welcome of the Leopard of Wilama who is coming on a state visit next month.

STUDENT: *(By way of intervention)* Why do you think the former Minister or Finance disappeared? He was the only member of the Cabinet opposed to their evil plans.

The crowd goes wild with a roar of protest ... Enter six helmeted policemen, carrying rifles and belts of cartridges, bedecked with canisters of different shapes and sizes. They file noisily past the auditorium, stopping at the approaches of the stage. The Inspector marches arrogantly on stage, megaphone in hand ... The crowd appears unmoved.

INSPECTOR: *(Through his megaphone)* I hereby put it to you that your gathering here is a contravention of the state of emergency of Yanke, and of Decree Number Nine Thousand six hundred and eighty five banning all demonstrations, processions, gatherings, etc. etc. etc. in Yanke. *(Pause)* I hereby order you to disperse in the name of the Lion of Yanke, President for Life, Commander-in-Chief of the Armed Forces, the one and only Conqueror of the British Empire, Husband of a Thousand Women, Terror of Youth ...

The Policeman's order only serves to infuriate the crowd who break into chants and songs:

How many people police go kill o?
How many people soldier go kill?
Them go shoot us tire
Them go kill us tire o
How many people soldier go kill?

How many people soldier go shoot o?
How many people police go shoot
We go show them fire
We go show them fire
How many people soldier go kill?

Defied, the Inspector orders his men on stage. They fan out and take aim. A moment later, six bodies including those of two policemen lie silent on the stage. Old man is one of them. Shouts and wails. Lights fade to black.

Act V

Demonstrators and the Police frozen in semi-darkness, spotlight falls on Narrator as he walks towards the stage through one of the aisles of the auditorium. He arrives stage centre, talks directly to the audience. There is solemnity and confidence in his voice, but not bitterness.

NARRATOR: *E kuu joko oo.* Thank you for sitting so patiently while we acted out a piece of dream. Yes, it is a dream now, with its masks and painted faces, its props and parables. But it is a dream plucked from the rust and dust of our streets, from the tinsel glitter of powerful thrones. *(Pause)* Who says there is something wrong with dreams, positive dreams? What is reality if not the shadow of a dream, what is idea if not the maturation of ideal ... *(Pauses, looks straight at the audience, nods his head in a sagely fashion)*

What you have just seen is a short chapter in a l-o-n-g dream. The people have shown their anger; the guns have answered. *(Pointing behind him)* The outcome is so dramatically obvious. *(Pause)* But Yankeland will never be the same again. In every village, every hamlet, the questions raised here are fledgeling into birds which perch on every roof. Questions too many for the steel muzzle of the gun. The days of the Lion are severely numbered.

(With all emphasis) There is something in the human spirit that guns *cannot* kill ...

What you have just seen is a small fragment of an unfolding dream. This drama goes beyond the curtain call. This play does not end here.

Thank you again. *E ki 'le o.*

Off-stage, an outburst of chants, louder, fuller, more defiant than ever before.

A slow blackout.

Glossary of translations

p. 10　　Classy Mercedes, king of cars
　　　　The one who glides noiselessly into the house of the affluent,
　　　　Enemy of the poor;
　　　　Classy Mercedes, shake your waist beads
　　　　The one with copious buttocks like those of a veteran concubine
　　　　The Mercedes has eyes, who says it doesn't?
　　　　Didn't it see the household of the poor
　　　　Before going the way of the rich?
　　　　The wretched who doesn't clear the way for the Benz
　　　　Is only courting a speedy death
　　　　Who doesn't know that whoever is crushed by
　　　　Mercedes tyres
　　　　Is a thousand times luckier than one killed by a Tortoise (that is, Volkswagen)
　　　　Rather than die a miserable death
　　　　May the good Lord find me rest under Mercedes tyres.

p. 16, line 5:　For the eyes not to see evil, the legs are the cure
　　　　　　　(If the eyes are not to see evil, the legs must be fast)

p. 16, line 7:　My Head, the entire body is the cure!

p. 18, line 4:　*ewi* (poetry, verse)

p. 20, line 12:　*O tooo!* (Enough!)

p. 22, line 12:　Alas, hunger has come!

p. 30, line 12:　*iro* (also called wrapper; a piece of cloth wrapped around the lower part of the body by women); *buba* (a blouse-like top piece worn above the *iro*)

p. 30, line 16: The money you've given to us

p. 30, line 17: No thief can snatch it

p. 43, line 13: Thank you, Baba; may you live long so you can utter more proverbs!

p. 43, line 15: *gele* (headgear worn by women)

p. 48, line 3: Pari killed what? (A Yoruba-induced play on the words in the French phrase)

p. 53, line 25: Alas! Taboo!

p. 56, line 16: Most extraordinary! Mighty Masquerade!

p. 64, line 29: Greetings to all at home.

Undoubtedly one of the world's most significant contemporary poets, Niyi Osundare has authored over ten volumes of poetry, two selected volumes, four plays, and numerous essays on African literature and culture. A strong believer in poetry as performance and the need for the oral animation of the word, he has performed his poetry in different parts of Africa, Asia, Europe, Canada, and the United States; and his poems have been translated into French, Dutch, German, Spanish, Italian, Japanese, and Korean.

A well-regarded and much decorated poet, Osundare has won several national and international awards, including the Association of Nigerian Authors (ANA) Poetry Prize, the ANA/Cadbury Poetry Prize (twice), the Commonwealth Poetry Prize, and the Noma Award, Africa's most prestigious book award. In 1998 he was recipient of the Fonlon/Nichols Award for "excellence in literary creativity combined with significant contributions to Human Rights in Africa". A year later, he was conferred with an honorary doctorate by the University of Toulouse-Le Mirail in France.

Professor and former Head, Department of English, University of Ibadan, he is also Professor of English at the University of New Orleans, U.S.A.

Born in Ikere-Ekiti in 1947, he was educated at the Universities of Ibadan, Leeds, and York, in Toronto, Canada.

www.ingramcontent.com/pod-product-compliance
Lightning Source LLC
Chambersburg PA
CBHW010742170426
43193CB00018BA/2918